COUPLE'S REPORT CARD

WEEKLY/MONTHLY
ASSESSMENT

DR. CHARLES QUINN

authorHOUSE®

AuthorHouse™
1663 Liberty Drive
Bloomington, IN 47403
www.authorhouse.com
Phone: 833-262-8899

Published by AuthorHouse 08/13/2024

ISBN: 979-8-8230-2921-6 (sc)
ISBN: 979-8-8230-2920-9 (e)

Library of Congress Control Number: 2024912893

WEEKLY/MONTHLY
COUPLE'S REPORT CARD

The Couple's Report Card

The Couple's Report Card is a gentle reminder that identifies areas of strengths and weaknesses within a relationship. It allows each person to become an accountability partner by grading their partner's weekly or monthly relational-interactions (RI), while also reflecting on their own RI.

This weekly/monthly report card will identify areas of positive progress or repeated troublesome patterns within the relationship while giving constructive criticism (please remember, constructive criticism should be encouraging and uplifting).

When giving feedback, it is important to remain respectful, loving, considerate, and nonjudgmental or non-accusatory. Finally, it allows partners to celebrate progress as they grow together.

HOW TO USE THIS REPORT CARD

First, select whether it will be a 'Weekly' or 'Monthly' assessment by circling. Next, read each question/ statement carefully as you reflect on your partner throughout the past week/month's involvement. Then decide what letter grade you would rate their relational interaction. Check box "A" for 'Amazing' efforts put forth by your partner or check box "B" if your partner's actions have gotten better, check box "C" for areas where they need to 'Consider some Corrections' in areas you have discussed in a prior constructive conversation or check box "I" for 'Improvements needed (maybe even an Intervention)', which, the improvements will be written out in a constructive, and non-threatening way. This will be listed in another section on the Report Card. Please remember when grading your partner, you are here to build, encourage,

and empower each other. Please do not use this as a weapon to provoke fear, obligation, or guilt (fog), push away, or emasculate.

An overall Growing and Giving Personal-Affection (GPA) rating will be given after the grading process has been conducted.

Self-Evaluation: A Self-Evaluation is also conducted with the same Report Card. You get to grade your own weekly or monthly actions, as well. This section is designed for you to take ownership of your actions or non-actions as it assists you in becoming a better version of yourself for you and your partner. This is your 'Gentle-Reminder' to treat with TLC two of your most prized possessions; your partner and yourself.

NAME:	DATE:	GPA (GROWING & GIVING - PERSONAL- AFFECTION) OVERALL RATING (1.0 – 10.0): _____.

Grade your partner with an A (Amazing),

B (Better), C (Consider-Corrections), or

I (*Improvement-needed),

*provide improvement feedback.

	[A].	[B].	[C].	[I].
a. Has my partner expressed my love-language this week/ month?				

	[A].	[B].	[C].	[I].
b. Has my partner supported me in any domestic chores this week/month?				
c. Has my partner's conversation been engaging and uplifting? (See note 1)				
d. Has my partner made me feel loved?				
e. My partner values my opinion and I feel heard when we conversate.				
f. Has my partner made me feel appreciated?				

	[A].	[B].	[C].	[I].
g. Has my partner made me feel safe and secure this week/month?				
h. Has my partner made any efforts to touch me this week/month?				
i. Has my partner said, "I love you" this week/month?				
j. Has my partner done anything special for me this week/month?				
k. My partner made good financial decisions this week/month?				

	[A].	[B].	[C].	[I].
l. My partner helped me be the best me/ feel fulfilled/reach my potential this week/ month?				
m. Has my partner made any effort to kiss and hug me?				
n. Has my partner made me feel like an equal this week/month?				
o. My partner has prioritized Quality Time with me this week/ month.				
p. Was my partner considerate and showed empathy?				

	[A].	[B].	[C].	[I].
q. My partner can receive constructive criticism without getting upset, retaliating, or justifying themselves.				
r. Has my partner been open and honest with me this week/month?				
s. My partner has been sexually fulfilling and made me feel wanted and desirable.				
t. Has my partner showed family commitment this week/month?				

	[A].	[B].	[C].	[I].
u. My partner is staying physically and mentally healthy. They seek self-improvement.				
v. Has my partner been attentive to my Emotional Needs? (see note 2)				
w. Has my partner been present with me and not distracted by other things?				
x. My partner knows my likes, dislikes, aspirations, expectations, and stressors.				

	[A].	[B].	[C].	[I].
y. My partner does not belittle me, especially in front of others, or berate me with others.				
z. My humble and loving suggestions for my partner are: _____ _____ _____ _____ _____ _____ _____ _____ _____.				

SELF-EVALUATION REPORT CARD WEEKLY/MONTHLY

A (Amazing), B (Better),

C (Consider-Corrections), or

I (*Improvement-needed),

*Provide improvement feedback.

NAME:	DATE:	GPA (GROWING & GIVING - PERSONAL- AFFECTION) OVERALL RATING (1.0 – 10.0): _____.

* Please place a letter grade in each box

	[A].	[B].	[C].	[I].
a. Have I made any effort to speak my partner's love-language?				
b. Have I made any efforts to support in any of the domestic chores?				

	[A].	[B].	[C].	[I].
c. Has my conversation been engaging and uplifting?				
d. Have I been there this week for my partner?				
e. Have I made smart financial decisions or contributed financially to the family?				
f. Did I show respect to my partner this week/ month?				
g. Have I made my partner feel loved this week/month?				

	[A].	[B].	[C].	[I].
h. Have I been present and actively listening to my partner?				
i. Have I complained a lot this week/month: (No=A or B) (Yes=C or I)				
j. Have I been self-focused or engaging with my partner? (engaged=A or B)				
k. Have I told my partner, "I love you" this week/month?				
l. Have I done anything special for my partner this week/month?				

	[A].	[B].	[C].	[I].
m. Have I been blaming my partner this week/ month? (No=A or B)				
n. Have I been supporting my partner's goals/ dreams?				
o. Have I kissed and hugged my partner this week/month?				
p. Have I been present (emotionally/physically) when my partner needed me?				
q. Have I made any efforts to take my partner on a date? (Yes = A or B/ No = C or I)				

	[A].	[B].	[C].	[I].
r. During conflicts/ issues with my partner, did I respond with consideration and sensitivity?				
s. Have I been taking care of my physical appearance this week?				
t. During conflicts, I employed problem-solving skills and techniques instead of getting angry. (Yes = A or B/ No = C or I)				
u. During a problem, did we work together as a team or as opponents?				

	[A].	[B].	[C].	[I].
v. Did I respond to my partner's needs with understanding, attentiveness, and sensitivity?				
w. Did I attempt to understand my partner's perspective on issues:				
x. Did I listen to my partner's perspective without victimizing myself or pointing the finger?				
y. Are there any offense, passive aggression, resentment, or unforgiveness? (No = A or B/ Yes = C or I)				

	[A].	[B].	[C].	[I].
z. Things I need to work on are: _____ _____ _____ _____ _____ _____ _____ _____ _____.				

MY ISSUES/ CONCERNS:	POSITIVE THINGS SEEN:	MY EXPECTATIONS:

OUR FUTURE GOALS:	OUR NEXT DATE NIGHT IS:	WHAT I DESIRE:
	_____	
	_____	
	_____	
	_____	
	_____	
	_____.	
	OUR NEXT VACATION TOGETHER IS:	
	_____	
	_____	
	_____	
	_____	
	_____	
	_____.	

_____

_____

_____

_____

_____

_____

_____

_____

_____

_____

_____

_____

_____

_____

_____

_____

Note 1

Some tips for Intimate Conversations

1. Put into words what you are feeling, regardless of how it may sound.
2. Ask your partner open-ended questions.
3. Make exploratory statements to help discover your partner's feelings and needs.
4. Express patience, consideration, empathy, and understanding towards your partner.
5. Separate light/fun conversations from the more serious ones.
6. Pick Up on Nonverbal Cues.
7. Don't Try to Read Their Mind.
8. Be mindful of your tone.
9. Find the right time to Talk.
10. Tell your partner what you need from them.
11. Validate your partner's emotions.
12. Create a safe space for your partner to express what they feel.
13. Never stop flirting with your partner.
14. Show active listening skills, by eye contact, turn toward your partner, and give feedback.

Note 2

Emotional Needs

Emotional Needs are feelings or conditions we need to feel happy, fulfilled, or at peace. When these needs are not met, we may feel frustrated, easily agitated, hurt, or dissatisfied. There are 10 core Emotional Needs within Relationships, in which we have primarily three of these needs. (Abraham Maslow, 1943)

1. Affection*. 2. Acceptance. 3. Trust. 4. Validation. 5. Autonomy. 6. Security. 7. Empathy. 8. Prioritization. 9. Privacy 10. Connection.

WEEKLY/MONTHLY
COUPLE'S REPORT CARD

The Couple's Report Card

The Couple's Report Card is a gentle reminder that identifies areas of strengths and weaknesses within a relationship. It allows each person to become an accountability partner by grading their partner's weekly or monthly relational-interactions (RI), while also reflecting on their own RI.

This weekly/monthly report card will identify areas of positive progress or repeated troublesome patterns within the relationship while giving constructive criticism (please remember, constructive criticism should be encouraging and uplifting).

When giving feedback, it is important to remain respectful, loving, considerate, and nonjudgmental or non-accusatory. Finally, it allows partners to celebrate progress as they grow together.

HOW TO USE THIS REPORT CARD

First, select whether it will be a 'Weekly' or 'Monthly' assessment by circling. Next, read each question/statement carefully as you reflect on your partner throughout the past week/month's involvement. Then decide what letter grade you would rate their relational interaction. Check box "A" for 'Amazing' efforts put forth by your partner or check box "B" if your partner's actions have gotten better, check box "C" for areas where they need to 'Consider some Corrections' in areas you have discussed in a prior constructive conversation or check box "I" for 'Improvements needed (maybe even an Intervention)', which, the improvements will be written out in a constructive, and non-threatening way. This will be listed in another section on the Report Card. Please remember when grading your partner, you are here to build, encourage,

and empower each other. Please do not use this as a weapon to provoke fear, obligation, or guilt (fog), push away, or emasculate.

An overall Growing and Giving Personal-Affection (GPA) rating will be given after the grading process has been conducted.

Self-Evaluation: A Self-Evaluation is also conducted with the same Report Card. You get to grade your own weekly or monthly actions, as well. This section is designed for you to take ownership of your actions or non-actions as it assists you in becoming a better version of yourself for you and your partner. This is your 'Gentle-Reminder' to treat with TLC two of your most prized possessions; your partner and yourself.

NAME:	DATE:	GPA (GROWING & GIVING - PERSONAL-AFFECTION) OVERALL RATING (1.0 – 10.0): _____.

Grade your partner with an A (Amazing),

B (Better), C (Consider-Corrections), or

I (*Improvement-needed),

*provide improvement feedback.

	[A].	[B].	[C].	[I].
a. Has my partner expressed my love-language this week/ month?				

	[A].	[B].	[C].	[I].
b. Has my partner supported me in any domestic chores this week/month?				
c. Has my partner's conversation been engaging and uplifting? (See note 1)				
d. Has my partner made me feel loved?				
e. My partner values my opinion and I feel heard when we conversate.				
f. Has my partner made me feel appreciated?				

	[A].	[B].	[C].	[I].
g. Has my partner made me feel safe and secure this week/month?				
h. Has my partner made any efforts to touch me this week/month?				
i. Has my partner said, "I love you" this week/month?				
j. Has my partner done anything special for me this week/month?				
k. My partner made good financial decisions this week/month?				

	[A].	[B].	[C].	[I].
l. My partner helped me be the best me/ feel fulfilled/reach my potential this week/ month?				
m. Has my partner made any effort to kiss and hug me?				
n. Has my partner made me feel like an equal this week/month?				
o. My partner has prioritized Quality Time with me this week/ month.				
p. Was my partner considerate and showed empathy?				

	[A].	[B].	[C].	[I].
q. My partner can receive constructive criticism without getting upset, retaliating, or justifying themselves.				
r. Has my partner been open and honest with me this week/month?				
s. My partner has been sexually fulfilling and made me feel wanted and desirable.				
t. Has my partner showed family commitment this week/month?				

	[A].	[B].	[C].	[I].
u. My partner is staying physically and mentally healthy. They seek self-improvement.				
v. Has my partner been attentive to my Emotional Needs? (see note 2)				
w. Has my partner been present with me and not distracted by other things?				
x. My partner knows my likes, dislikes, aspirations, expectations, and stressors.				

	[A].	[B].	[C].	[I].
y. My partner does not belittle me, especially in front of others, or berate me with others.				
z. My humble and loving suggestions for my partner are: _____ _____ _____ _____ _____ _____ _____ _____ _____.				

SELF-EVALUATION REPORT CARD WEEKLY/MONTHLY

A (Amazing), B (Better),

C (Consider-Corrections), or

I (*Improvement-needed),

*Provide improvement feedback.

NAME:	DATE:	GPA (GROWING & GIVING - PERSONAL-AFFECTION) OVERALL RATING (1.0 – 10.0): _____.

* Please place a letter grade in each box

	[A].	[B].	[C].	[I].
a. Have I made any effort to speak my partner's love-language?				
b. Have I made any efforts to support in any of the domestic chores?				

	[A].	[B].	[C].	[I].
c. Has my conversation been engaging and uplifting?				
d. Have I been there this week for my partner?				
e. Have I made smart financial decisions or contributed financially to the family?				
f. Did I show respect to my partner this week/month?				
g. Have I made my partner feel loved this week/month?				

	[A].	[B].	[C].	[I].
h. Have I been present and actively listening to my partner?				
i. Have I complained a lot this week/month: (No=A or B) (Yes=C or I)				
j. Have I been self-focused or engaging with my partner? (engaged=A or B)				
k. Have I told my partner, "I love you" this week/month?				
l. Have I done anything special for my partner this week/month?				

	[A].	[B].	[C].	[I].
m. Have I been blaming my partner this week/ month? (No=A or B)				
n. Have I been supporting my partner's goals/ dreams?				
o. Have I kissed and hugged my partner this week/month?				
p. Have I been present (emotionally/physically) when my partner needed me?				
q. Have I made any efforts to take my partner on a date? (Yes = A or B/ No = C or I)				

	[A].	[B].	[C].	[I].
r. During conflicts/ issues with my partner, did I respond with consideration and sensitivity?				
s. Have I been taking care of my physical appearance this week?				
t. During conflicts, I employed problem-solving skills and techniques instead of getting angry. (Yes = A or B/ No = C or I)				
u. During a problem, did we work together as a team or as opponents?				

	[A].	[B].	[C].	[I].
v. Did I respond to my partner's needs with understanding, attentiveness, and sensitivity?				
w. Did I attempt to understand my partner's perspective on issues:				
x. Did I listen to my partner's perspective without victimizing myself or pointing the finger?				
y. Are there any offense, passive aggression, resentment, or unforgiveness? (No = A or B/ Yes = C or I)				

	[A].	[B].	[C].	[I].
z. Things I need to work on are: _____ _____ _____ _____ _____ _____ _____ _____ _____ .				

MY ISSUES/ CONCERNS:	POSITIVE THINGS SEEN:	MY EXPECTATIONS:

OUR FUTURE GOALS:	OUR NEXT DATE NIGHT IS:	WHAT I DESIRE:
	_____	
	_____	
	_____	
	_____	
	_____	
	_____.	
	OUR NEXT VACATION TOGETHER IS:	
	_____	
	_____	
	_____	
	_____	
	_____	
	_____.	

Note 1

Some tips for Intimate Conversations

1. Put into words what you are feeling, regardless of how it may sound.
2. Ask your partner open-ended questions.
3. Make exploratory statements to help discover your partner's feelings and needs.
4. Express patience, consideration, empathy, and understanding towards your partner.
5. Separate light/fun conversations from the more serious ones.
6. Pick Up on Nonverbal Cues.
7. Don't Try to Read Their Mind.
8. Be mindful of your tone.
9. Find the right time to Talk.
10. Tell your partner what you need from them.
11. Validate your partner's emotions.
12. Create a safe space for your partner to express what they feel.
13. Never stop flirting with your partner.
14. Show active listening skills, by eye contact, turn toward your partner, and give feedback.

Note 2

Emotional Needs

Emotional Needs are feelings or conditions we need to feel happy, fulfilled, or at peace. When these needs are not met, we may feel frustrated, easily agitated, hurt, or dissatisfied. There are 10 core Emotional Needs within Relationships, in which we have primarily three of these needs. (Abraham Maslow, 1943)

1. Affection*. 2. Acceptance. 3. Trust. 4. Validation. 5. Autonomy. 6. Security. 7. Empathy. 8. Prioritization. 9. Privacy 10. Connection.

WEEKLY/MONTHLY COUPLE'S REPORT CARD

The Couple's Report Card

The Couple's Report Card is a gentle reminder that identifies areas of strengths and weaknesses within a relationship. It allows each person to become an accountability partner by grading their partner's weekly or monthly relational-interactions (RI), while also reflecting on their own RI.

This weekly/monthly report card will identify areas of positive progress or repeated troublesome patterns within the relationship while giving constructive criticism (please remember, constructive criticism should be encouraging and uplifting).

When giving feedback, it is important to remain respectful, loving, considerate, and nonjudgmental or non-accusatory. Finally, it allows partners to celebrate progress as they grow together.

HOW TO USE THIS REPORT CARD

First, select whether it will be a 'Weekly' or 'Monthly' assessment by circling. Next, read each question/statement carefully as you reflect on your partner throughout the past week/month's involvement. Then decide what letter grade you would rate their relational interaction. Check box "A" for 'Amazing' efforts put forth by your partner or check box "B" if your partner's actions have gotten better, check box "C" for areas where they need to 'Consider some Corrections' in areas you have discussed in a prior constructive conversation or check box "I" for 'Improvements needed (maybe even an Intervention)', which, the improvements will be written out in a constructive, and non-threatening way. This will be listed in another section on the Report Card. Please remember when grading your partner, you are here to build, encourage,

and empower each other. Please do not use this as a weapon to provoke fear, obligation, or guilt (fog), push away, or emasculate.

An overall Growing and Giving Personal-Affection (GPA) rating will be given after the grading process has been conducted.

Self-Evaluation: A Self-Evaluation is also conducted with the same Report Card. You get to grade your own weekly or monthly actions, as well. This section is designed for you to take ownership of your actions or non-actions as it assists you in becoming a better version of yourself for you and your partner. This is your 'Gentle-Reminder' to treat with TLC two of your most prized possessions; your partner and yourself.

NAME:	DATE:	GPA (GROWING & GIVING - PERSONAL-AFFECTION) OVERALL RATING (1.0 – 10.0): _____.

Grade your partner with an A (Amazing),

B (Better), C (Consider-Corrections), or

I (*Improvement-needed),

*provide improvement feedback.

	[A].	[B].	[C].	[I].
a. Has my partner expressed my love-language this week/month?				

	[A].	[B].	[C].	[I].
b. Has my partner supported me in any domestic chores this week/month?				
c. Has my partner's conversation been engaging and uplifting? (See note 1)				
d. Has my partner made me feel loved?				
e. My partner values my opinion and I feel heard when we conversate.				
f. Has my partner made me feel appreciated?				

	[A].	[B].	[C].	[I].
g. Has my partner made me feel safe and secure this week/month?				
h. Has my partner made any efforts to touch me this week/month?				
i. Has my partner said, "I love you" this week/month?				
j. Has my partner done anything special for me this week/month?				
k. My partner made good financial decisions this week/month?				

	[A].	[B].	[C].	[I].
l. My partner helped me be the best me/ feel fulfilled/reach my potential this week/ month?				
m. Has my partner made any effort to kiss and hug me?				
n. Has my partner made me feel like an equal this week/month?				
o. My partner has prioritized Quality Time with me this week/ month.				
p. Was my partner considerate and showed empathy?				

	[A].	[B].	[C].	[I].
q. My partner can receive constructive criticism without getting upset, retaliating, or justifying themselves.				
r. Has my partner been open and honest with me this week/month?				
s. My partner has been sexually fulfilling and made me feel wanted and desirable.				
t. Has my partner showed family commitment this week/month?				

	[A].	[B].	[C].	[I].
u. My partner is staying physically and mentally healthy. They seek self-improvement.				
v. Has my partner been attentive to my Emotional Needs? (see note 2)				
w. Has my partner been present with me and not distracted by other things?				
x. My partner knows my likes, dislikes, aspirations, expectations, and stressors.				

	[A].	[B].	[C].	[I].
y. My partner does not belittle me, especially in front of others, or berate me with others.				
z. My humble and loving suggestions for my partner are: _____ _____ _____ _____ _____ _____ _____ _____ _____ .				

SELF-EVALUATION REPORT CARD WEEKLY/MONTHLY

A (Amazing), B (Better),

C (Consider-Corrections), or

I (*Improvement-needed),

*Provide improvement feedback.

NAME:	DATE:	GPA (GROWING & GIVING - PERSONAL- AFFECTION) OVERALL RATING (1.0 – 10.0): _____.

* Please place a letter grade in each box

	[A].	[B].	[C].	[I].
a. Have I made any effort to speak my partner's love-language?				
b. Have I made any efforts to support in any of the domestic chores?				

	[A].	[B].	[C].	[I].
c. Has my conversation been engaging and uplifting?				
d. Have I been there this week for my partner?				
e. Have I made smart financial decisions or contributed financially to the family?				
f. Did I show respect to my partner this week/month?				
g. Have I made my partner feel loved this week/month?				

	[A].	[B].	[C].	[I].
h. Have I been present and actively listening to my partner?				
i. Have I complained a lot this week/month: (No=A or B) (Yes=C or I)				
j. Have I been self-focused or engaging with my partner? (engaged=A or B)				
k. Have I told my partner, "I love you" this week/ month?				
l. Have I done anything special for my partner this week/month?				

	[A].	[B].	[C].	[I].
m. Have I been blaming my partner this week/month? (No=A or B)				
n. Have I been supporting my partner's goals/dreams?				
o. Have I kissed and hugged my partner this week/month?				
p. Have I been present (emotionally/physically) when my partner needed me?				
q. Have I made any efforts to take my partner on a date? (Yes = A or B/ No = C or I)				

	[A].	[B].	[C].	[I].
r. During conflicts/ issues with my partner, did I respond with consideration and sensitivity?				
s. Have I been taking care of my physical appearance this week?				
t. During conflicts, I employed problem-solving skills and techniques instead of getting angry. (Yes = A or B/ No = C or I)				
u. During a problem, did we work together as a team or as opponents?				

	[A].	[B].	[C].	[I].
v. Did I respond to my partner's needs with understanding, attentiveness, and sensitivity?				
w. Did I attempt to understand my partner's perspective on issues:				
x. Did I listen to my partner's perspective without victimizing myself or pointing the finger?				
y. Are there any offense, passive aggression, resentment, or unforgiveness? (No = A or B/ Yes = C or I)				

	[A].	[B].	[C].	[I].
z. Things I need to work on are: _____ _____ _____ _____ _____ _____ _____ _____ _____.				

MY ISSUES/ CONCERNS:	POSITIVE THINGS SEEN:	MY EXPECTATIONS:

OUR FUTURE GOALS:	OUR NEXT DATE NIGHT IS:	WHAT I DESIRE:
	_____	
	_____	
	_____	
	_____	
	_____	
	_____.	
	OUR NEXT VACATION TOGETHER IS:	
	_____	
	_____	
	_____	
	_____	
	_____	
	_____.	

Note 1

Some tips for Intimate Conversations

1. Put into words what you are feeling, regardless of how it may sound.
2. Ask your partner open-ended questions.
3. Make exploratory statements to help discover your partner's feelings and needs.
4. Express patience, consideration, empathy, and understanding towards your partner.
5. Separate light/fun conversations from the more serious ones.
6. Pick Up on Nonverbal Cues.
7. Don't Try to Read Their Mind.
8. Be mindful of your tone.
9. Find the right time to Talk.
10. Tell your partner what you need from them.
11. Validate your partner's emotions.
12. Create a safe space for your partner to express what they feel.
13. Never stop flirting with your partner.
14. Show active listening skills, by eye contact, turn toward your partner, and give feedback.

Note 2

Emotional Needs

Emotional Needs are feelings or conditions we need to feel happy, fulfilled, or at peace. When these needs are not met, we may feel frustrated, easily agitated, hurt, or dissatisfied. There are 10 core Emotional Needs within Relationships, in which we have primarily three of these needs. (Abraham Maslow, 1943)

1. Affection*. 2. Acceptance. 3. Trust. 4. Validation. 5. Autonomy. 6. Security. 7. Empathy. 8. Prioritization. 9. Privacy 10. Connection.

SPECIAL THANKS TO

MY LOVELY WIFE, R. BONITA QUINN

Ms. Jacqueline K. Henry

Naheemah McMicheaux McCallop

Derek & Frida "T" Tillman

Printed in the United States
by Baker & Taylor Publisher Services